Original title:
The Laughing Leaves

Copyright © 2025 Creative Arts Management OÜ
All rights reserved.

Author: Giselle Montgomery
ISBN HARDBACK: 978-1-80567-449-8
ISBN PAPERBACK: 978-1-80567-748-2

Mirth in the Midst of Change

In the breeze, the whispers flow,
Silly tales of seeds that grow.
Spinning round in sunlight's glow,
Nature laughs, a playful show.

The branches sway, they twist and bend,
Tickling air, a giggling friend.
With every shift, the stories blend,
Jokes of seasons never end.

Serenade of the Amber Shades

Golden hues beam through the trees,
Leaves dance gently, flapping ease.
With every rustle comes a tease,
Nature's song brings heartfelt wheeze.

The shadows flicker, bright and bold,
Whimsy weaves its tales of old.
Underneath, the joy unfolds,
Each chuckle, a treasure to hold.

Cheerful Murmurs in the Forest

Rustling leaves in playful cheer,
Chirping birds lend hand to ear.
Echoes bouncing, loud and clear,
Laughter rings from far and near.

Each flower grins, a gentle sigh,
Nature winks as clouds float by.
In this realm where spirits fly,
Smiles abound like butterflies.

Chuckles Amongst the Oak and Maple

Amidst tall trunks, a secret lies,
Giggles spring from nature's eyes.
Branches tickle, teasing skies,
Laughter bursts, as color flies.

Maples murmur jokes with flair,
Oaks return with wise old air.
In this green realm, fun to share,
Joyful whispers fill the air.

Vibrant Giggles in the Wooded Wonderland

In a grove where humor plays,
The trees wear smiles on sunlit days.
Their whispers dance in playful cheer,
As branches sway, it's all so clear.

Beneath a sky of twinkling light,
The critters join, what a delight!
Squirrels tease the passing breeze,
While birds crack jokes with perfect ease.

Flowers chuckle in vibrant hues,
Tickled by the joyful views.
With every rustle, laughter grows,
As nature revels in its shows.

In this land where giggles bloom,
Even shadows can't contain the room.
A woodland filled with joy and glee,
Oh, what a funny place to be!

Exultation Among the Changing Branches

In a world where branches sway,
The trees seem jester-like today.
With every rustle, joy abounds,
And laughter swirls in silly sounds.

Even the mossy rocks agree,
Their chuckles bounce like a bumblebee.
The gentle breeze plays games of tag,
While leaves perform a happy wag.

With colorful blooms that beam so bright,
They paint the woods in pure delight.
Mighty oaks and wispy pines,
Share whimsical tales in joyful lines.

In the heart of the vibrant glen,
Laughter beckons, come join the fun.
Among the branches, smiles unite,
Celebrating life under the light!

Corners of Cheer in the Canopy

In the shade where shadows play,
Laughter bounces, bright and gay.
A squirrel twirls, a dance so spry,
While birds crack jokes that float on high.

Breezes tease with gentle sighs,
Whispering secrets, nature's spies.
A playful breeze, a ticklish leaf,
Together they weave their joyful brief.

Giggles in the Glistening Glades

Glades aglow with shimmer bright,
 Caterpillars giggle, a silly sight.
 Flowers toss their heads in glee,
 Each petal shares a funny spree.

Rabbits hop with bouncing tails,
 Telling tales of windy gales.
The brook chuckles, bubbling free,
 A melody of hilarity.

Jolly Images of the Fall Fest

Pumpkins grin from every patch,
Corn stalks wiggle, a harvest match.
Children chase the bright confetti,
While the scarecrows dance, looking ready.

Cider flows with frothy cheer,
Candied apples draw us near.
Balloons lift with giggly squeals,
As joyful laughter spins like reels.

Chipper Challenges Under the Chill

Chilly air brings a cheeky grin,
Frosty breath makes spirits spin.
Snowflakes flutter, swirling by,
Each one laughing as it flies.

Sleds provide a sassy race,
While cheeks blush in a rosy lace.
Wrap up warm and join the fun,
Together we'll chase the winter sun.

Playful Petals and Sunny Smiles

In the breeze, they sway and dance,
Colors twirl, oh what a chance!
Flitting here, they tease the air,
Joyful giggles everywhere.

Chasing shadows, bright and bold,
Sunshine stories to be told.
Petals wink with glee, they sway,
Nature's jesters, come out to play!

Sunlit Laughter Among the Branches

Branches stretch with arms so wide,
Sunshine tickles, feels like a ride.
Chirping birds join in the fun,
Under the rays, we laugh and run.

Squirrels giggle, chasing fast,
Among the leaves, shadows cast.
A playful breeze, a gentle tease,
Nature's laughter in the trees.

Frolics in the Forest Hideaway

Deep in woods where secrets hide,
Flowers play, they do not bide.
Whispers tickle the forest floor,
Every rustle brings out more.

Bumbles buzz and jump around,
Mr. Frog leaps with a bound.
With every hop, they make a scene,
Jokes from nature's lively green.

A Chorus of Cheery Colors

Each hue sings a silly tune,
Bouncing under the silver moon.
Dancing petals, side to side,
With every giggle, they take pride.

Together in a joyful band,
Colors chuckle, hand in hand.
Nature's palette, full of cheer,
A merry chorus, loud and clear.

Smiling Shadows on a Sunlit Path

In the golden light they play,
Shadows twisting, bright and gay.
A giggle in the rustling grass,
While little critters quickly pass.

Sunbeams twirl like merry sprites,
Chasing dreams through painted sights.
Each step whispers silly rhymes,
As laughter dances with the times.

Gleeful Whispers in the Swaying Branches.

Tickling air, the branches sway,
With secrets shared in breezy play.
Laughter echoes through the trees,
As nature joins in joyous tease.

The leaves chuckle, fluttering high,
Underneath a bright blue sky.
Every rustle brings a cheer,
As if the woods can truly hear.

Whispers of Golden Canopies

The treetops chatter, bright and bold,
In hues of amber, red, and gold.
They gossip low, then burst with glee,
Creating laughter, wild and free.

With every breeze, a punchline flies,
As nature cracks its jovial guise.
The sunlit stage, a leafy floor,
Where even silence holds a roar.

Dancing in the Autumn Breeze

Each twig a partner in the dance,
In the breeze, they spin and prance.
A whimsical waltz begins anew,
As wind tickles all it blows through.

The air is filled with playful jokes,
Among the trees, the laughter pokes.
With every leaf a playful wink,
In this swirl of joy, we sink.

Laughter Echoing Through the Glade

In the woods where shadows play,
Silly whispers lead the way.
Branches sway and giggles rise,
Nature's jokes under bright skies.

The sunbeam's tickle, a playful tease,
Rustling secrets among the trees.
A breeze carries chuckles near,
Echoes of joy for all to hear.

Amusement Among the Twirling Leaves

Round and round they twirl with glee,
Bouncing like the bumblebee.
Every gust, a new surprise,
Spinning humor beneath the skies.

Capers danced upon the ground,
Nature's laughter all around.
A leaf slips by with a wink,
Causing giggles, quick as you think.

Serendipity in the Swaying Shade

Underneath the leafy quilt,
Joy is sewn where fun is spilt.
A feathered friend joins the play,
Joking in its chirpy way.

Unexpected laughter flows,
As shadows sway and friendship grows.
Sunshine beams with playful light,
Dancing leaves in sheer delight.

Foliage Fables of Fun

Stories told through rustling hues,
Giggling gossip in every breeze.
Fables whispered among the trees,
Tickling tales that set hearts at ease.

Wink and nod, the branches sway,
Comedy blooms in a leafy ballet.
Every shade a chuckle brought,
With nature's humor, laughter's caught.

Jovial Jingles in the Leafy Labyrinth

In the twisty paths of green,
Laughter bubbles, bright and keen.
Branches dance, a playful spree,
Nature's giggles, wild and free.

Critters prance, they know the tune,
Flitting fast, like July's moon.
A squirrel dons a tiny hat,
While birds chirp, and danced they sat.

Rustling jokes in every tree,
Whispers shared, just you and me.
Dewdrops jingle, morning cheer,
In this maze, we laugh, sincere.

With every turn, a jest unfolds,
The wise old oak with tales retolds.
In this maze of joy we roam,
Each giggle feels like coming home.

Follies of the Flourishing Flora

A daisy winks, a tulip sings,
While in the breeze, a jest she flings.
The roses blush at what they hear,
As petals tickle, laughter's near.

In the garden, mischief blooms,
Jolly jests amid the plumes.
Bee in a tie, and quite a sight,
Buzzing jokes from morn till night.

Sunlight peeks with playful beams,
Chasing shadows, weaving dreams.
What blooms here is pure delight,
Nature's folly, so bright, so light.

The lilacs laugh, the lilies cheer,
As laughter bubbles, loud and clear.
In this plot of joy we find,
The blooming giggles, intertwined.

Jolly Interludes in the Arboreal Aisles

Beneath the boughs where giggles flow,
In dances bright, the breezes blow.
Whimsical vines twist and play,
Spinning tales of a sunny day.

A chipmunk jigs on a fallen branch,
While critters join in jovial dance.
Acorns tumble with raucous glee,
Nature's jesters, wild and free.

Every leaf a story tells,
Of funny antics in the dells.
Shadows laugh, in playful chase,
A merry world, a giddy place.

In wooded aisles, the fun abounds,
With silly echoes, laughter sounds.
Together here, we skip, we sway,
In this arboreal cabaret.

Merry Melodies of Nature's Tapestry

In weavings bright of green and gold,
Nature hums, with tales retold.
Fluffy clouds pass, tease the sun,
Their whispers weave a world of fun.

Bubbly brooks sing with delight,
Riffing laughs from day to night.
Curly ferns clap, twirling round,
In this symphony, joy is found.

At twilight's glow, the crickets play,
With strums of cheer, they join the fray.
A dance of shadows starts to sway,
As giggles drift on breezy bay.

Under starlit skies, so vast,
The moon joins in, her jokes are cast.
Together in this mirthful spree,
Nature's laughter sets us free.

Breezy Banter Among the Branches

In the trees, where chatter flows,
Laughter dances, and joy grows.
Squirrels giggle, twigs they tease,
Nature's jest, such merry breeze.

Birds swap jokes in cheerful tones,
Rustling leaves join in the groans.
Amidst the boughs, fun fills the air,
Whispers tickle without a care.

Frolicsome winds, a playful play,
Branch to branch, they skip and sway.
Even shadows start to grin,
While nature's jesters spread the din.

Whirling Whispers on the Wind

Through the fields, a breezy jest,
Whirling whispers never rest.
Tickling grasses, wild and free,
Tales of joy in harmony.

Dandelions puff and tease,
Sending giggles on the breeze.
Round and round, the petals fly,
Chasing clouds across the sky.

Sunlight dances on the ground,
With each chuckle, mirth is found.
Every gust brings tales anew,
As laughter blows right past you.

Happiness in the Harvest Hues

In fields aglow with golden zest,
All around, a lively fest.
Pumpkins chuckle, apples sway,
In hues of joy that light the day.

Carrots giggle, swaying bold,
While corn cobs tell tales of old.
Colors burst in playful glee,
Harvest time, so wild and free.

Cheerful echoes fill the air,
Nature's joy, beyond compare.
Every turn brings smiles anew,
In vibrant tones, the laughter grew.

Giggling in the Grassy Nooks

In the nooks where soft grass grows,
Whispers of fun and laughter flows.
Ladybugs laugh on blades so steep,
While tiny flowers giggle and peep.

Bumblebees buzz with a light tune,
Swaying to the sun and moon.
In green retreats, the chuckles play,
As joyful critters frolic away.

Softly, shadows hide and seek,
In the grass, the laughter's peak.
Rustling softly, joys ignite,
In playful nooks, all feels right.

Delightful Drifts of Golden Tresses

Golden curls in the air,
They twirl and dance with flair.
They giggle when the wind blows,
Swaying gently, joy bestows.

Chasing shadows, playing games,
Whispering sweet little names.
Sunshine laughs, the world agrees,
Nature's charm puts hearts at ease.

Ticklish breezes tease the ground,
In this frolic, laughter's found.
Floating whispers, secrets share,
Woven magic everywhere.

Spin around, the day's a delight,
Dancing wildly till the night.
With each twist, we find our beat,
Nature's jesters, oh so sweet.

Sassy Breezes and Chirping Leaves

Sassy winds that tease and play,
Fluttering leaves in bright array.
Chirps of laughter fill the sky,
As the breezes flit and fly.

Leaves exchange their cheeky tales,
Rustling softly with the gales.
Jests and jives in perfect sync,
Nature's wits make spirits wink.

Breezy banter, light and spry,
Swirling whispers, oh so sly.
Every twist and turn they take,
Silly paths in giggles wake.

Boundless joy beneath the trees,
Sassy murmurs in the breeze.
Nature's laughter, pure and bright,
Makes our hearts take joyful flight.

Lively Tales from the Treetops

Treetops speak in rustling tones,
Telling tales of bouncing cones.
Squirrels giggle, birds all sing,
Bouncing lightly on a wing.

Whimsical stories spin and sway,
In the sunlight, bright and gay.
With each flutter, dandelions twirl,
Nature's mischief in a whirl.

Branches sway with cheeky glee,
Every movement hints at spree.
Tales of fun in every leaf,
Brimming over with belief.

Curious whispers fill the air,
Lively secrets everywhere.
Dancing shadows, laughter's hold,
With each story, joys unfold.

Joyous Journeys in the Heart of the Woods

In the woods where laughter twirls,
Joyful journeys, rhythm swirls.
Each step taken, light and free,
Bouncing hearts, like a spree.

Cheerful echoes call and play,
Creatures joining in the fray.
Every footfall, a delight,
Nature's party feels just right.

Sunbeams dance on leaf and path,
Whisking us to joy and laugh.
With every sight, a chuckle bright,
In this wonder, hearts take flight.

Adventures bloom where laughter grows,
In a symphony of prose.
Playful spirits, ever bold,
In the woods, our tales unfold.

Tickle of the Wind Through Verdant Canopies

Whispers dance with a playful breeze,
Branches sway with a giggling tease.
Sunlight flickers, shadows play,
Nature's jesters brightening the day.

Swaying limbs in a jolly spin,
Rustling tales where chuckles begin.
Tickling leaves sing a merry tune,
Under the watch of the chuckling moon.

Every flutter brings a cheer,
A flutter of fun for all to hear.
With each gust, a new delight,
Laughter lingers in the light.

In this grove, joy takes flight,
Where breezy giggles fill the night.
Such mischief in the green can gleam,
Life's a comedy, pure as a dream.

Amusement Under the Arboreal Arch

Under arches of leafy cheer,
Nature paints smiles far and near.
Capering critters chasing fun,
A carnival in the warming sun.

Branches bend with whispers sweet,
While squirrel acrobats take their seat.
Twigs crackle with a playful sound,
Where laughter of trees can be found.

With every gust, a howl of glee,
Dancing shadows on the spree.
Their humor echoes through the glade,
In this leafy masquerade.

Echoed laughter in the trees,
Sprinkling joy with every breeze.
A canopy of mirth and light,
Where happiness takes to flight.

Bright Banter from the Boughs

Above the ground, the branches chat,
In gentle tones, like chittering chat.
Each rustling leaf shares a tale,
Of playful winds that never fail.

Lively voices stir the air,
Jokes and jests without a care.
The boughs a-burst with laughter's grace,
A canopy of humor's embrace.

Capping off the day with fun,
As shadows lengthen, webs are spun.
The sun dips low, the giggles bloom,
Nature's stage is never gloom.

Join the uproar, lift your gaze,
Find the joy in woodland maze.
With every leaf, let laughter soar,
In the forest's heart, forever more.

Spirited Smiles from the Skies

When clouds parade in frolicsome strands,
The sun dips low, and joy expands.
Brisk breezes weave a light surprise,
With spirited smiles from azure skies.

Raindrops giggle on green attire,
Nature dances in pure desire.
Each drop a sigh, a playful tease,
Sprinkling joy with the greatest ease.

The horizon blushes, sharing delight,
As day fades softly, bidding good night.
Stars peek out with a twinkling grin,
Under their watch, all fun begins.

So lift your head, embrace the game,
Where laughter blossoms, never the same.
In every moment, joy persists,
Nature's laughter, a gentle twist.

Merry Whirls in the Woodland

In the forest, leaves take flight,
Spinning round in pure delight.
Branches chuckle, roots get wise,
Nature's pranks in bright disguise.

Squirrels dance a tuneful jig,
While the rabbits laugh and dig.
Wind blows softly, whispers tease,
Every rustle, fun to seize.

Each acorn drops with silly flair,
Causing giggles everywhere.
Mushrooms pop with laughter's tone,
In this place, we're never alone.

Frogs play peek-a-boo in streams,
Chasing bubbles, sharing dreams.
Joyful echoes fill the air,
Woodland humor everywhere.

Folly Among the Ever-changing Foliage

Leaves in shades of yellow, green,
Flip and twirl like a playful scene.
Whispers crackle through the trees,
Folly dances with the breeze.

Every rustling leaf has jest,
Tickling squirrels, loving best.
Branches sway in silly tunes,
Playing games 'neath glowing moons.

Brightly colored, leaves confide,
Secrets floating in the tide.
Glimmers twinkle, laughter stirs,
Nature's joy, as life occurs.

Tumbling twigs and leafy grins,
Whimsical antics where joy begins.
From summer's song to autumn's cheer,
Folly reigns, bringing us near.

Elation in the Eaves

Up above, the branches sway,
Giggles drift and dance each day.
Little critters scurry 'round,
Under eaves, where glee is found.

Birds compose a cheeky tune,
Softly laughing with the moon.
Winks exchanged from twig to leaf,
Nature's joy, beyond belief.

Raindrops fall like bouncing balls,
Creating laughter 'neath the walls.
In cozy corners, whispers play,
Delightful moments on display.

Sunshine peeks with every beam,
Crafting warmth, igniting dream.
The eaves echo with playful cheer,
In this realm, there's naught to fear.

Grinning Vistas of the Verdant

A tapestry of green unfurls,
Bright with laughter, nature swirls.
Fields of joy stretch far and wide,
In verdant slopes, we laugh and glide.

Whimsical winds lead the way,
Tickling grasses in their play.
Flowers giggle, petals bright,
Painting smiles with pure delight.

Clouds in shapes of silly beasts,
Floating by, hosting strange feasts.
Laughter bubbles from the streams,
Where joy hums as sunlight beams.

Every corner sways with glee,
Nature's laughter, wild and free.
With grinning vistas all around,
In this happy world, we're found.

Hilarity of the Harvest Moon

Beneath the moon so bright and round,
The creatures gather, joy abound.
A raccoon juggles autumn treats,
While chipmunks dance on tiny feet.

The pumpkins smile, with grins so wide,
As squirrels slide down to glide.
The breeze whispers a humorous tune,
Brought forth by the harvest moon.

All around, the jokes take flight,
As owls hoot with pure delight.
The shadows play, a silly play,
On this most comical, quirky day.

So gather round, all who delight,
In laughter 'neath the starry night.
With winks and nods, our hearts take flight,
Under the hilarity of the night.

Kooky Kisses from the Canopy

The branches sway in playful cheer,
With giggles echoing, loud and clear.
The leaves play tag, a breezy game,
  Each rustle whispers a silly name.

Down below, the shadows dance,
While breezes twirl in a merry prance.
A squirrel winks, with nuts in tow,
  As sunlight kisses with a glow.

The flowers grin, their colors bright,
In a waltz of whimsy, pure delight.
With every bud, a chuckle springs,
As nature laughs and joyfully sings.

So let us join this canopy,
In funny moments, wild and free.
With kooky kisses all around,
In nature's humor, joy is found.

Exuberance in the Evolving Treetops

In the treetops where laughter sways,
The birds exchange their silly plays.
A parrot laughs, a crow responds,
In this orchestra of funny bonds.

The branches wave, a playful scene,
As squirrels act like they've unseen.
A raccoon prances, full of glee,
Sipping sunlight, like it's tea.

The leaves, they giggle in twilight's hue,
Sprinkling joy like morning dew.
In every gust, a jest unfolds,
In every whisper, a story told.

The vibrant greens do leap and bound,
A celebration, oh, nature's sound!
In evolving treetops high and grand,
Exuberance spreads through every strand.

Smiling Roots and Rejoicing Blooms

In gardens deep, where roots reside,
They chuckle softly, filled with pride.
Each petal sways, a happy tune,
As flowers wink beneath the moon.

The daisies giggle, in the sun's embrace,
While tulips twirl with such a grace.
A bumblebee buzzes a funny song,
In this patch where we all belong.

The herbs share secrets, gentle and nice,
Each sprout brings forth a little spice.
As laughter bubbles from the ground,
In smiling roots, joy can be found.

So here we gather, all in bloom,
In this cheerful, fragrant room.
With every giggle that goes 'round,
Rejoicing blooms in laughter's sound.

Radiant Laughter of Nature

In the breeze, the branches sway,
Whispering secrets, come what may.
Every twig a jester bright,
Tickling the air with pure delight.

Bubbles of sunshine dance and peek,
Nature's giggles play hide and seek.
A rustle here, a chuckle there,
Joyful echoes fill the air.

Up above, the skies burst wide,
Clouds like clowns in a fun ride.
With every gust, a playful shout,
Nature's humor all about.

So let us stroll through fields and trees,
Where laughter rides upon the breeze.
Each leaf a smile, each flower a grin,
Laughter of worlds, where fun begins.

Silly Shadows of the Swirling Thicket

Dancing in circles, shadows play,
Giggling softly, they're here to stay.
Branches twist in a comical way,
As sunlight makes the silly sway.

Squirrels leap with acrobatic flair,
Chasing their tails without a care.
The thicket chuckles with every sound,
Life's funny antics all around.

Mice play pranks and frogs join in,
With splashes and hops, a joyful din.
Each rustling leaf has a story to tell,
Of moments that linger, a spell to dispel.

So let's embrace this playful scene,
Where every corner has teeny beans.
Fun spills over, both wild and free,
In the swirling thicket, come laugh with me.

Playful Spirits of the Grove

In the grove, the spirits roam,
With giggles light as a feathered foam.
They dance on branches, jump on breeze,
Spreading delight with playful ease.

A rustle here, a wink over there,
Their laughter flows in the open air.
With every flick, they tease and spin,
Inviting us to join their din.

Flowers blush in colors bright,
Responding to the joyful flight.
Bubbles of joy among the trees,
Sparkling laughter in every tease.

So take a step into this mirth,
Feel the joy that fills the earth.
In the grove where hearts can sing,
Every moment's a joyous fling.

Glee in the Shades of September

As autumn whispers with a cheeky grin,
The air is ripe with joyful din.
Leaves tumble down like confetti tossed,
In this game of joy, we are never lost.

Colors clash in a jubilant fight,
Each leaf a dancer in golden light.
Breezes play tag with the warming sun,
In September's lap, pure fun's never done.

Squirrels chuckle, scampering near,
Gathering treasures without any fear.
The moments sparkle, tickling the earth,
In laughter's presence, we find our mirth.

So let's celebrate this grand parade,
Where shadows dance and colors invade.
In the shades of September, let's all partake,
In the glee of nature, for laughter's sake.

Vivid Vignettes of the Leafy Laughs

In the breeze, they dance and twirl,
Whispering jokes, a secret swirl.
Each flutter brings a chuckle near,
Nature's humor, light and clear.

Swaying branches playfully tease,
Joking with soft, rustling ease.
Cozy shadows giggle bright,
Underneath, the sun takes flight.

Colors burst with playful cheer,
Rustling laughter fills the air.
A comedy in every hue,
Nature smiles, both bold and true.

From golden crowns to emerald sprees,
Funny whispers among the trees.
In every branch, a punchline sprouts,
A tapestry of giggles flouts.

Jests on a Golden Trail

On paths adorned with nature's gold,
Stories of silliness unfold.
Leaves erupt in laughter bright,
Tickling toes in morning light.

In a waltz, the colors play,
Making mischief, come what may.
Beneath the oak, a silly game,
Shadows poke and tease the same.

Wsnickers wash through swaying boughs,
Nature's jesters take their bows.
A rustle, a crinkle, a playful cheer,
Each leaf a comedian, ever near.

With every step, the laughter grows,
Golden jests from roots to toes.
On this path, the world's a stage,
Where each leaf writes a joyous page.

Sundrenched Smiles of the Trees

Beneath the sun, the branches grin,
As breezes push and pull them in.
Every sunbeam, a playful jest,
Nature's laughter, at its best.

With every rustle, chuckles rise,
In leafy laughter, sweet surprise.
Gold and green in a merry fray,
Whispering secrets throughout the day.

Leaves spin round in bright delight,
Tickling the air like pure sunlight.
Each wayward gust brings forth a cheer,
Laughter echoes, crystal clear.

Climbing high in sunny embrace,
All trees share a funny face.
Among them, joy is never far,
Each leaf glittering like a star.

Cackling Cascades of Color

In a whirl of hues, the laughter flies,
Splashing joy beneath the skies.
Each leaf a dancer, full of grace,
Brimming with mischief, a bright embrace.

Amidst the shades, the giggles bloom,
Casting away all shades of gloom.
In every bend, a twist of cheer,
Colors cascade, winking near.

Golden laughter spills on ground,
As joyful echoes spin around.
With rustling whispers, they conspire,
Creating raucous mirth, a choir.

Every branch, a playful muse,
Sharing tales of funny ruse.
In a riot of colors; what's the chance?
Nature's jesters lead the dance.

Sneaky Chuckles Under the Starlit Sky

In the quiet of the night,
Whispers bounce with pure delight.
Stars above play peek-a-boo,
While shadows dance, just me and you.

Branches sway with hidden glee,
Tickling tricks from every tree.
Moonlit laughter fills the air,
As nature joins in without a care.

Winks and giggles from afar,
Beneath the light of a shining star.
Rustling softly, a gentle tease,
Nature's humor puts us at ease.

So come and tread on dew-kissed ground,
Where every stump tells jokes profound.
In the dark there's mischief rife,
As we share this joyful life.

Frothy Fun of the Nature Trail

Bubbles rise from the brook's flow,
Frogs croak jokes, putting on a show.
Sunshine dances on the leaves,
As playful breezes play tricks and tease.

Every step brings sounds of cheer,
Rusty giggles tickle the ear.
Chipmunks dart with acorn snacks,
Plotting chuckles, and playful acts.

Mushrooms giggle in their rows,
While daisies whisper what they know.
The path ahead is filled with fun,
In this grand nature's prankster run.

So wander forth where laughter leads,
Among the flora, nature speeds.
Find frothy fun in every hue,
As the world around joins in too.

Raucous Revelations in the Arbor

Branches sway in a merry tune,
Chirping birds in the afternoon.
Every leaf has a tale to spin,
With a wink, let the laughter begin.

A squirrel giggles as he leaps,
Hiding nuts, in playful heaps.
Beneath the shade, the secrets flow,
With every breeze, the fun will grow.

Raucous roots and merry vines,
Spouting witticisms like fine wines.
Whispering breezes burst with cheer,
Nature's jesters always near.

So let the game of chuckles start,
As joyful sounds fill every heart.
In this lively scene where we belong,
Each raucous revelation sings a song.

Gracious Grins from the Greening World

Every bud holds a cheeky grin,
In the grass where the giggles begin.
Petals flutter, each a tease,
Nature's charm will sure appease.

Fields of green with laughter rife,
Inviting joy into our life.
Blossoms bloom in vibrant show,
As breezes dance and tickle low.

Joyful whispers on gentle streams,
Echoes of our sweetest dreams.
With every rustle, a chuckle calls,
As we wander past the garden walls.

So feel the fun that nature brings,
In this world of gracious things.
Unlock the joy that surely swirls,
In laughter's arms, the greening world.

Boisterous Bliss of the Blushing Boughs

Swaying branches dance and jive,
Chortling as the breezes thrive.
Colorful whispers rustle and play,
Tickling laughter in a frolicsome sway.

With vibrant hues that tickle the eye,
They cheerfully shimmy and seemingly fly.
Giggling shadows upon the ground,
Spinning joy with each swaying sound.

Boughs of mirth in dizzying spins,
Heartfelt chuckles as the fun begins.
Up in the air, leaping high,
As nature's wits paint the blue sky.

What a sight to behold in the trees,
Nature's jesters swaying with ease.
Echoing giggles all around,
In this grand show where cheer is found.

Merry Mosaics of Fall's Foliage

Bursts of colors, a quirky blend,
Leaves in laughter, they twist and bend.
Jubilant murmurs and giggles ensue,
Crafting a scene that's silly and new.

Crimson and gold in a silly parade,
Every flap and flutter a prankster trade.
Nudging each other on gusts of delight,
Chasing the sun till the day turns to night.

Whirling in circles, they show no shame,
Fooling the passerby, playing a game.
Here is a hue that winks with glee,
Spreading smiles from tree to tree.

A tapestry woven in playful fun,
Where jokers abound, and laughter's begun.
As autumn giggles and prances along,
In this whimsical waltz, we all belong.

Ecstatic Eddies in the Elm

Under the branches where breezes squawk,
Leaves are giggling and starting to talk.
Round and round they swirl like a fuss,
Creating a ruckus, they laugh and discuss.

Dancing in circles, they whisper with flair,
Bouncing about without a care.
In this vibrant frenzy of shades so bright,
Each playful flutter brings pure delight.

Gusts carrying chuckles through the air,
Nature's own jesters, without a care.
Swinging and twirling, they charge and retreat,
Sparking joy at your dancing feet.

As branches sway in a jovial tease,
The elms crack jokes in the playful breeze.
With every rustle, a giggle takes flight,
In the wild waltz of the day and night.

Whims of the Wind in Whirling Trees

The wind plays tricks, with a twist and a turn,
  Leaves take the bait and giggle and churn.
  In a carousel dance, they flutter and glide,
  Tickled by breezes, they laugh and collide.

With every gust, a story unfolds,
Whispers of mischief, each tree's heart bold.
  A bouquet of laughter in every sway,
    Turning the ordinary into play.

They prance with glee, these leafy pranksters,
  In nature's theater, they are the bankers.
For when the wind whispers its funny refrain,
  The trees respond with joy and with gain.

What marvels await in this joke-filled show,
  As branches bounce and the breezes blow.
  A carnival of colors, a chatty ballet,
In the whims of the wind, we all want to stay.

Whispers of Joyful Foliage

In the breeze, they flutter, a cheeky dance,
Branches shake and giggles prance.
Whirling colors, a playful show,
Nature's laughter, steal the glow.

Underneath the sun's warm gleam,
Leaves share secrets, a funny dream.
Rustling whispers in the air,
Every moment's a joyful flare.

Twisting, twirling, and spinning around,
A symphony of chuckles found.
With every sway, a chuckle grows,
In the sky, their laughter flows.

Dancing shadows upon the ground,
Leaves toss jokes that know no bounds.
Buddies in shades of green and gold,
Their merry tales are sweetly told.

Giggles in the Canopy

Up high where the sunlight gleams,
The leaves exchange their funny dreams.
A rustle here, a waggle there,
Laughter weaves through fragrant air.

Swinging from branches, oh what a sight,
Bubbling giggles in morning light.
A ticklish breeze through emerald rows,
Caressing tales that nobody knows.

Each leaf's a storyteller bold,
Unraveling secrets of days gone old.
Flip and flop in a breezy game,
These mirthful moments, never the same.

Giggling shadows dance on the ground,
As nature's laughter pairs with sound.
Joyful tunes in the canopy's embrace,
Every sway is a smiling face.

Dancing with the Autumn Breeze

Autumn whispers with a wiggly tune,
Leaves skitter and dip, like a happy cartoon.
Golden and crimson, they twirl and spin,
A playful jig as the breezes begin.

Round and round in the cool, fresh air,
Lively chortles float everywhere.
They know how to sway and tease,
As they sway and slosh with joyful ease.

Bouncing lightly from tree to tree,
Making merry, feeling so free.
Each gust of wind, a chuckling friend,
Creating moments that never end.

With rustling whispers, stories unfold,
Through every twirl, adventures are told.
So let's join the fun, come take this chance,
To dance with the leaves in a jolly romance.

Serenade of the Swaying Trees

In a fragrant grove where the tall trees sway,
The leaves croon songs in a funny ballet.
Bending and bowing to playful beats,
Nature's concert in sunny retreats.

Nutty giggles drift on the breeze,
Chiming laughter from the swaying leaves.
They brush against each other in glee,
A melody of joy, wild and free.

Creeping shadows dance on the ground,
With every rustle, new delights found.
Each levity-filled moment we share,
Is a tune of laughter woven in air.

So listen closely to the rustling sounds,
Where joy and silliness knows no bounds.
Each leaf a singer, a jester they seem,
Creating a world woven from a dream.

Jest of the Colorful Boughs

In the breeze, the branches sway,
Tickling time in a playful way.
Whispers of giggles in the air,
As nature chuckles without a care.

Bright orange, yellow, and cheerful green,
Dancing together like a lively scene.
They skip and jump on gentle winds,
Nature's jesters, where joy begins.

With each rustle, the laughter grows,
Bright sunbeams light the leafy shows.
So come and join, don't hesitate,
In this boughs' party, let's celebrate!

Giggles abound in every nook,
Ticklish foliage, come take a look.
The trees tell tales with sways and bends,
Where the whispers of laughter never ends.

Whimsical Chatter of the Canopy

Above the ground, the branches talk,
As silly squirrels take a walk.
Leaves giggle when they brush and sway,
In a bright and breezy cabaret.

The sun peeks through with a catty grin,
While shadows dance, they twirl, they spin.
The laughter echoes, a soft parade,
In this leafy theater, life's charade.

Each branch a comedian in nature's play,
Telling secrets at the end of the day.
In a chorus of chuckles that fill the sky,
With curls and curls of mirth nearby.

Joyful leaves in their raucous bloom,
Carrying whispers that chase away gloom.
The air tastes bright with stories galore,
As laughter of the trees sings forevermore.

Frolic of the Flamboyant Forest

In a forest bright with trumpet sounds,
Where claptrap trees tease the ground.
Watch as the branches leap with glee,
A wild group dance, just come and see!

Chirpy birds join the frolic too,
Painting the air with skies so blue.
The bushes giggle and chime along,
Merry and bright in nature's song.

With a twist, a turn, a playful grin,
Each leaf spins tales where joy begins.
Come, twirl and swirl beneath the trees,
Wings and leaves dance to the breezy tease.

A canopy of laughter overhead,
As colors collide like confetti spread.
In this circuit of whimsy and cheer,
The flamboyant forest draws us near.

Humorous Hues in the Twilight

As dusk arrives, the colors jest,
With chuckles and giggles, they're at their best.
Faded reds and softening greens,
Paint the world in funny scenes.

The shadows stretch and begin to play,
As colors mingle in a wild ballet.
The sunset blushes, a rosy tease,
While whispers drift upon the breeze.

Tree tops chuckle in twilight's glow,
As fireflies twinkle a soft show.
Underneath this playful sky,
A carnival of giggles hints nearby.

In hues so humorous, the evening sighs,
Where laughter dances and never dies.
So linger a while as colors unite,
In joyful antics of the fading light.

Giggles of the Wind-Swept Trees

In the forest, whispers play,
Branches chuckle in their sway.
Tickling boughs, a breezy shout,
Nature's joy, without a doubt.

Frolicking leaves, a dance so bright,
With every gust, they take to flight.
Cackling wind, a merry tune,
As tree tops sway beneath the moon.

Rustling softly, a playful tease,
Bringing laughter on the breeze.
Nature's jesters, bold and free,
Chortling tales of glee and glee.

In their embrace, the shadows laugh,
Turning moments into art.
With every crinkle, giggles arise,
Celebrating life beneath the skies.

Joyful Rustles in a Sunlit Glen

In the meadow, colors beam,
Dancing leaves, a sunny dream.
Swaying lightly, under the glow,
Whispering secrets, soft and low.

Crickets chirp, a lively beat,
Grasshoppers jump to complete the feat.
Together they sing, a happy crew,
Making merry, like skies so blue.

Tickling twigs, they start to tease,
Shaking off the morning freeze.
Laughter echoes all around,
In this glen, joy is found.

Sun-kissed moments, laughter flows,
Where every petal, a giggle knows.
In this realm of light and cheer,
Each joyous rustle draws us near.

Chortles Beneath the Bark

Under canopies of green delight,
Life's shenanigans take flight.
Frolicking critters, a jovial crew,
Add to the fun, with antics anew.

Treetops giggle, branches sway,
Rustling laughs, in bright array.
Nature's humor all around,
In every crevice, giggles found.

Beneath the bark, a chuckle grows,
Silly whispers where no one knows.
Tickling roots and drumming leaves,
Crafting laughter, all it weaves.

As shadows dance and sunlight gleams,
Laughter echoes in sunny streams.
Joyful whispers play hide and seek,
Creating fun, as nature speaks.

Harmonies of Swaying Foliage

In the grove, a playful sound,
Where swaying fronds are joy unbound.
Laughter blooms with each soft sway,
    Harmony joins the lightest play.

Leaves shimmy, playful and bright,
In sun's embrace, they twirl with delight.
A giggle here, a chuckle there,
    Nature's music fills the air.

Swaying limbs in rhythmic dance,
Encourage smiles, invite romance.
Beneath their shade, we all find peace,
    A humor that never seems to cease.

Oh how they rustle, with gleeful sound,
    Telling tales of joy profound.
In this orchestra of the great outdoors,
    Laughter lives forevermore.

Jocular Rustle in the Woodland

In the woods where whispers play,
Branches bounce and branches sway.
Critters chuckle, dance around,
With every rustle, joy is found.

Squirrels jesting, tails held high,
Chasing shadows as they fly.
The sunbeams giggle through the trees,
A chorus of laughter on the breeze.

Witty winds blow, tickles ensue,
Leaves in harmony, bright and new.
Nature's jesters, all in glee,
Causing smiles like a jubilee.

Twinkling branches, a playful tease,
Echoing laughter that won't appease.
In this woodland, fun's the call,
Joyful rustling, enchanting all.

Glee Among the Glades

In the glades where giggles grow,
Sunlight dances, soft and slow.
Tiny flowers burst with cheer,
Nature's laughter we hold dear.

Butterflies flutter, mock a chase,
Each petal spins, a funny place.
The grass sways, wants to play,
In this haven, joy's at bay.

A brook chuckles, bubbles bright,
Winking waters, pure delight.
Every tickle from a breeze,
Brings a chuckle with such ease.

Chirping birds with silly songs,
Join in, make merry throngs.
In the glades, with laughter rife,
Every moment is a slice of life.

Radiance of the Reveling Roots

Beneath the ground, roots twist and spin,
Whispers bubble, let joy in.
They wiggle, laugh, dance in place,
A giggly party, what a space!

They share tales with the soil near,
In fun and frolic, nothing drear.
Each wiggle sends the earth alight,
Gleeful antics in the night.

Mirthful creatures join the show,
Their happy grins like rainbows glow.
Roots delight in every jest,
In this earthy, giggly fest.

Together they create a song,
In this rooty realm, we belong.
Laughter echoes through the ground,
A joyous riddle all around.

Merry Melodies of the Meadow

In the meadow, laughter rises,
Where croaking frogs give sly surprises.
The daisies dance, a merry bunch,
Filling hearts like a cheerful lunch.

Grasshoppers sing, in playful beats,
Twirling around on tiny feet.
The sun snickers, tickling leaves,
While nature tells what it believes.

Every bloom wears a smile bright,
Bobbing heads in sheer delight.
With every breeze, the fun expands,
A tapestry of joyful lands.

Winding paths of giggles trail,
In the meadow, no room to fail.
With laughter shared, the day is won,
A canvas painted, light and fun.

Lively Legends of Leafy Laughter

In the garden, whispers play,
Tiny tales of light and sway.
Each leaf chuckles, green and bright,
Dancing shadows, pure delight.

Squirrels giggle up above,
Chasing dreams, just like a dove.
Breezes tease, a playful song,
Nature grins, where all belong.

The daisies bloom, quite absurd,
Tickled pink, they hardly heard.
In this world of roots and cheer,
Every rustle brings good cheer.

So step outside, let laughter ring,
Join the chorus, feel the spring.
For every leaf, a story spun,
A joyous life, where all is fun.

Jumpy Joy in the Ferns

Underneath the ferns so bright,
Jumping jacks in pure delight.
Each frond swings, oh what a sight,
Tiny dancers, day and night.

With every turn, they leap and bounce,
Nature's whimsy starts to louse.
Crickets chirp, a beat so sweet,
Frogs all join, tapping their feet.

The ladybugs parade around,
In their spots, no solemn frown.
With every hop and gleeful cheer,
They paint the air with laughter here.

So come along, and take a chance,
In the ferns, let's join the dance.
With every rustle, joy appears,
A funny world that calms all fears.

Bouncing Spirits of the Dappled Understory

In the shade where shadows roam,
Bouncing spirits make their home.
Lurking giggles in the vine,
Tickling tales, oh how they shine.

Each leaf flips, a playful tease,
Whirling whispers on the breeze.
Laughter echoes, swift and free,
Nature's jesters, can't you see?

The mushrooms wiggle, dressed in cheer,
Winking as you wander near.
Beneath the boughs, let joy unfold,
Funny secrets waiting, bold.

So take a stroll, with heart in hand,
In the dappled, laughing land.
With every step, a chuckle peaks,
Join the fun that nature seeks!

Revelations in the Radiant Retreat

In a haven, bright and warm,
Laughter dances, free from harm.
Sunlight dapples, joy will bloom,
Nature's secrets lift the gloom.

Butterflies with vibrant grace,
Wingeled twirls in this embrace.
The flowers giggle, colors flash,
Chasing shadows in a dash.

The stream bubbles, teasing low,
'Come and play!' it starts to flow.
Each ripple hums a funny tune,
Beneath the light of afternoon.

So revel here, in humor's glow,
Join the laughter, let it grow.
A radiant retreat we find,
With every leaf, a smile aligned.

Joyful Journeys in the Autumn Light

Golden whispers tickle the breeze,
Swaying branches dance with ease.
Critters giggle in chase and race,
Nature's playground, a cheerful space.

Puddles splash with every leap,
Joyful secrets this day will keep.
Bouncing leaves, they twirl and spin,
In this funny game, we all can win.

Laughter drifts on the autumn air,
Frolicsome chatter, light and rare.
Chasing shadows, a silly show,
In this circus, the wild winds blow.

With every step, delight abounds,
In this world where joy resounds.
Skip along the winding stream,
Embrace the laughter, live the dream.

Chirping Cheer of the Canopy

Up in the trees, the chatter flows,
Banters of birds in funny clothes.
Leaves gossip with a rustling cheer,
Tickling laughter for all to hear.

A squirrel slips with a playful dive,
Chasing friends as they come alive.
Nutty jokes from branches high,
Spreading smiles 'neath the bright blue sky.

Fluttering wings, a playful ballet,
Bouncing beats that sway and play.
In this giggling green parade,
Joyful echoes will never fade.

Rays shimmer through the leafy dome,
Every branch feels just like home.
With every chirp, a silly rhyme,
In this canopy, it's always prime.

Lifted Spirits in the Lushness

In the thicket where laughter blooms,
Funny whispers chase away glooms.
Bouncing buds with a vibrant flair,
Jolly echoes dance in the air.

Gentle breezes giggle along,
As colors burst in nature's song.
Chasing shadows, we run amok,
In this vivid realm, tickled by luck.

Bumbling bees do a jig and twirl,
Funny antics make the heart whirl.
Every glade seems to chuckle around,
With every giggle, joy can be found.

So come join the frolicsome spree,
Where laughter reigns wild and free.
In the lushness, we awaken the glee,
A funny world, just you and me.

Tittering Under the Twilight

As daylight fades, shadows convene,
With a soft sparkle, the world's unseen.
Whispers flutter like tiny wings,
A little laughter in twilight sings.

The moon peeks shyly, a watchful friend,
Lighting giggles that never end.
Breezy chuckles through the night,
In the glow, everything feels right.

Gathered critters telling tales,
Unruly jests riding on the gales.
Under the stars, the fun expands,
Holding hands in whimsical bands.

So let the night be filled with cheer,
In this tittering wonder, we draw near.
Feel the warmth, let the laughter grow,
In twilight's grasp, we steal the show.

Euphoria in the Leafy Reflections

In the breeze, they wiggle and sway,
Joking with shadows, come out to play.
Whispers of mirth dance here and there,
Tickling the sun with a witty air.

Around each bend, a chuckle grows,
Beneath broad branches, laughter flows.
Silly shadows with faces so bright,
Turning the day into sheer delight.

With every rustle, a wink is shared,
Nature's own jesters, perfectly paired.
Giggles over petals like bursts of cheer,
Echoes of joy for all who can hear.

Merriment hides in dappled shades,
Under the canopy, the humor cascades.
A whimsical world where the giggles reign,
Euphoria blooms like a joyous stain.

Gleeful Glades of Change

In vibrant realms where daylight beams,
The trees conspire with pickled dreams.
Branches bend low, each leaf a grin,
Sparkling secrets flutter, woven thin.

Golden rays play, a trickster's delight,
Poking fun at shadows, banishing fright.
Gales carry whispers of laughter anew,
Transforming the glades in colors so true.

Sway and giggle, the roots do shake,
Over every fool's path, the fairies break.
Embracing the change, in glee we roam,
In these joking woods, we find our home.

Jubilant frolic where time's lost its way,
In gleeful glades where we frolic and play.
Each rustle a riddle, each tree a tease,
Life's little laughter carried by the breeze.

Chipper Colors in the Forest

A kaleidoscope bursts in cheerful hues,
While leaves up top wear their playful shoes.
Giggling branches sway left and right,
Squirrels and songbirds join the delight.

Crinkly edges, a voice from above,
Crackling with laughter, so free, so in love.
Puffs of green and flashes of red,
Nature's jesters wearing crowns on their head.

Down in the underbrush, whispers ensue,
Tiny insects join in with a buzzing woo-hoo!
A parade of giggles, a carnival scene,
Every leaf shimmying in vivid sheen.

With each rustling melody, joy intertwines,
Completing the canvas with laughter's designs.
Chipper and bright, the forest is keen,
In nature's embrace, we dance and we dream.

Revelry in the Rustling Trees

On breezy paths where the zany meet,
Leaves spin tales, with laughter so sweet.
Every rustle reveals a surprising jest,
In the arms of nature, we feel truly blessed.

Beneath the bright canopies swaying free,
To the tune of the wind, oh what glee!
Silly dances erupt from the bark,
Shaking with smiles even after dark.

Lively whispers fly on a fizzy breeze,
Flirting with echoes through swaying trees.
Every creak's a giggle, every bend a cheer,
Nature's grand party is finally here!

Step light, laugh loud, come join in the spree,
Under the branches, feel young and carefree.
In the whimsy of woods, joy's found anew,
In revelry we wander, the forest our view.

Mirthful Murmurs of Nature

In the breeze, a giggle plays,
Rustling dresses for sunny days.
Branches sway with jest and cheer,
Nature's laughter ringing near.

Tiny critters dance around,
Tickled by the joyful sound.
With every rustle, trees conspire,
Spreading echoes full of fire.

Whispers of the grass join in,
Jokes shared from the roots to skin.
Frogs croak tunes of pure delight,
Underneath the moon's soft light.

A chorus sings from blooms so bright,
Painting mischief in the night.
Smiles abound in every crevice,
Nature's humor, oh so precious.

Chuckles Beneath the Boughs

Underneath the sprawling limbs,
Where shadow play and laughter swims.
Crickets chirp, while squirrels tease,
Communing with the buzzing bees.

Old oaks whisper silly tales,
As breezes blow and laughter sails.
Each rustle tells a joke well-known,
In the arms of trees, joy has grown.

Giggling fawns in meadows prance,
Entwined in joy, they laugh and dance.
Woodpeckers drum a humored beat,
Making mischief fun and sweet.

Clouds drift by with cheeky grins,
Dancing lightly, the fun begins.
Every rustling leaf and throng,
Calls the world to join the song.

Jests in the Greenery

Sunlight tickles blades so green,
Painted laughter on the scene.
Flowers share their cheeky quirks,
As playful nature slyly works.

Butterflies flutter, giggling loud,
Daring blooms to join the crowd.
Breezy whispers hold a jest,
In this merry, leafy fest.

Squirrels scamper with a grin,
Sharing secrets where they've been.
Mossy carpets hide their trails,
While wild melodies dance in gales.

Every thicket hums a rhyme,
Tickled by the hands of time.
Among the greenery, it's true,
Nature's jest is meant for you.

Echoes of Whimsy in the Grove

In quiet glades where shadows play,
Whimsy weaves throughout the day.
Trees bend low to share a grin,
Inviting all to let joy in.

Rabbits hop with laughter high,
Chasing clouds that drift on by.
In the rustle, a secret shared,
Hints of joy, lightly bared.

Petals flutter with playful glee,
A dazzling show for all to see.
Nature's palette, bright and bold,
Hides stories begging to be told.

As day bids night a fond goodbye,
The stars wink down from velvet sky.
Jokes of nature never cease,
In every moment, find your peace.

Whimsical Twirls of the Green Canopy

Breezes dance with sprightly flair,
Tickling branches in the air.
Sunlight giggles through the leaves,
Nature's laughter, oh, it weaves.

Swaying trees in playful jest,
Joking shadows never rest.
Whispers crackle, a merry sound,
In this realm, joy is found.

Acorns tumble, what a sight,
Crafting games in pure delight.
Rustling voices fill the day,
In this joyous, green ballet.

Gusts of wind, they share a wink,
Leaving smiles, one wouldn't think.
In the canopy, laughter grows,
With every twist, the fun just flows.

Radiant Revelry Among Nature's Bouquets

Petals giggle, colors bright,
A garden party, pure delight.
Bees are buzzing with their cheer,
Gathering nectar, spreading leer.

Tulips wink and daisies sway,
Inviting frolic into play.
Nature's canvas, bold and free,
A tapestry of glee.

Pansies chuckle, jolly ties,
Sun-kissed laughter fills the skies.
In this floral jubilee,
Every bloom joins merrily.

Petal dances, breezy flight,
Twinkling stars wink through the night.
Nature's laughter, rich and pure,
In each blossom, joy's allure.

Blissful Boughs and Fluttering Grins

Frilly branches, carefree spins,
Whisper secrets, cheeky grins.
Overhead, the critters cheer,
Celebrating life right here.

Chirps and caws, a merry tune,
Rustling leaves begin to croon.
Branch to branch, the giggles flow,
As the breezes play below.

Budded twigs with laughs we hear,
Twirling lightly, spreading cheer.
Every rustle tells a tale,
Full of joy, never stale.

Hopping squirrels join the scene,
Chasing shadows, quick and keen.
In this grove where mirth takes flight,
Every moment feels just right.

Vibrant Chortles in the Garden

In the garden, laughter blooms,
Frolic under bright, warm moons.
Dandelions tickle toes,
While the breezy mischief blows.

Cheerful petals, laughter bright,
Swirling 'round, a merry sight.
Butterflies with giggles glide,
Bumping blooms, side by side.

Sunshine whispers, a jolly call,
Nature hosting its grand ball.
Vibrant colors skip and swirl,
In this dance, hearts do twirl.

Every bud, a joke untold,
In the warmth, we break the mold.
As we gather, joy will spread,
In this haven, laugh instead.

www.ingramcontent.com/pod-product-compliance
Lightning Source LLC
Chambersburg PA
CBHW051653160426
43209CB00004B/884